Original title:
Lessons in Goodbye

Copyright © 2024 Swan Charm
All rights reserved.

Author: Linda Leevike
ISBN HARDBACK: 978-9916-89-955-7
ISBN PAPERBACK: 978-9916-89-956-4
ISBN EBOOK: 978-9916-89-957-1

## Finding Peace in the Goodbye

In silent halls, we part ways,
The echoes linger, memories blaze.
With heavy hearts, we bid adieu,
In faith, we trust, our paths renew.

The dawn will rise, our spirits soar,
In every tear, love's gentle roar.
God's hand will guide, a soft embrace,
In every ending, find your grace.

## A Journey into the Beyond

Through valleys deep, we wander on,
With whispered prayers, the night's not long.
The stars are lights to heavenly ways,
In every heart, the spirit stays.

The river flows, a sacred stream,
In every life, a woven dream.
We walk in faith, on paths unseen,
The journey leads, our souls redeemed.

## The Sacred Silence of Departures

In quiet moments, we reflect,
A sacred bond, a deep connect.
The whispers hush, the stillness calls,
In every soul, a love that brawls.

As shadows fade, the light shines bright,
In every end, a gracious light.
We hold the memories, let them flow,
In sacred silence, love will grow.

## In the Name of Letting Go

In whispered prayers, we learn to yield,
With open hearts, our wounds are healed.
Each moment passed, a fleeting grace,
In letting go, we find our place.

The strength to walk, to rise, to stand,
In every breath, we understand.
The spirit guides, a gentle breeze,
In love's embrace, we find our peace.

## **The Whispered Promises of Dusk**

In twilight's soft embrace we find,
Whispers of hope in shadows designed.
The stars align with purpose bright,
Guiding our souls through the night.

Promises linger in the fading light,
Cradled by angels, within their sight.
Each breath a prayer, our hearts ablaze,
In the warmth of dusk, our spirits raise.

The moon ascends, a beacon aloft,
Illuminating dreams, tender and soft.
We walk the path of sacred trust,
In shadows of dusk, we turn to dust.

## **The Path of Graceful Exits**

In every ending, grace gently lies,
A sacred journey where spirit flies.
Each step taken with reverent care,
Embracing the silence, whisper a prayer.

With open hearts, we face the dawn,
As memories echo, love is reborn.
The path stretches wide for those who roam,
In the light of departure, we find our home.

Salvation awaits at the gates of night,
Where souls unite in transcendent light.
With every farewell, a blessing unfolds,
Stories of wisdom in silence retold.

## In the Stillness of Letting Go

In the stillness, our spirit sighs,
Letting go of burdens, we rise.
Each tear a reminder of love's embrace,
Woven together in time and space.

With every heartache, new strength is born,
As we learn to dance with the dawn.
Fractured pieces become whole once more,
In the quiet, we find peace at our core.

The silence speaks in a sacred tone,
Guiding our hearts toward the unknown.
In the art of surrender, we find our way,
With faith as our compass, come what may.

## The Sacred Arc of Farewell

In the arc of goodbye, love does not fade,
Sacred connections, forever laid.
Each moment cherished, echoing grace,
A timeless bond, no distance can erase.

Let our hearts sing in unity's song,
Embracing the journey, where we belong.
In the farewell's glow, truth reveals,
The power of love, as the spirit heals.

Beneath the stars, we bid adieu,
Grateful for memories forever true.
In every heartbeat, we carry on,
In the sacred arc, we are never gone.

## **Heavy with Haloed Memories**

In the stillness, shadows loom,
Whispers echo, hearts in bloom.
Days of reverence, nights of prayer,
Each moment cherished, held with care.

Fingers trace the sacred lines,
Stories woven, love defines.
Through tears and laughter, faith remains,
A guiding light through joys and pains.

Time stands still, the past invoked,
In every breath, a promise spoke.
Memories haloed, bright and clear,
In holy warmth, we hold them dear.

## The Gentle Return to the Light

In the dawn, a soft embrace,
Bringing warmth to every place.
With open hearts, we find our way,
To grace and truth, in peace we stay.

Whispers of hope fill the air,
Guiding souls beyond despair.
Each step taken, a sacred rite,
Towards the gentle, golden light.

With every heartbeat, spirit soars,
As love unlocks celestial doors.
In laughter's echoes, joy ignites,
The gentle return to love's delights.

## **Where Sacrifice Meets Solitude**

In quiet corners, a broken heart,
Where sacrifice and silence part.
A heavy crown, the burden borne,
In solitude, a new hope's sworn.

Hands uplifted, prayers like streams,
Across the night, faith softly gleams.
Each sacrifice, a story told,
In the stillness, courage bold.

Through shadows deep, love's fire burns,
Where longing lingers, spirit yearns.
In solitude, the truth unfolds,
A testament of grace retold.

## The Divine Embrace of Absence

In every silence, a whisper found,
The divine presence all around.
Absence weighs like a sacred stone,
Yet in the void, we are not alone.

Hearts entwined in love's soft sighs,
Memories linger, never dies.
In absence, we seek the unseen hand,
To guide our steps upon this land.

With faith as lantern, we wander through,
The shadowed paths, a promise true.
In the embrace of absence, we rise,
Closer to heaven, beyond the skies.

## Finding Solace in Departure

In the silence of twilight's glow,
We seek the path where shadows flow.
With whispered prayers to guide our way,
We find the strength to face the day.

Hearts intertwined, though we must part,
In love's embrace, we make a start.
Each farewell holds a promise still,
A soft reminder of God's will.

Through sacred spaces, we shall tread,
Where memories linger, softly spread.
In every tear, a blessing found,
In every loss, our hearts unbound.

With open arms, we greet the night,
Where stars align in heaven's light.
In every ending, life renews,
We find our peace, a path we choose.

## Wings of Spirit in the Night

Beneath the veil of midnight skies,
The spirit soars where freedom lies.
In whispers soft, the silence sings,
A testament to all good things.

Through darkened woods and shadowed paths,
The heart remembers all it hath.
In dreams we rise, our hopes take flight,
Embracing grace in every night.

The moonlight bathes the weary soul,
In starlit grace, we are made whole.
With every breath, our spirits gleam,
In faith, we dance, we live, we dream.

For in the night, we find our guide,
In gentle nudges, love does abide.
With wings of spirit softly spread,
We learn to trust, as tears are shed.

## The Last Hymn of a Requiem

In solemn halls where echoes weep,
We gather close, our vigil keep.
With voices low, we raise a song,
A final hymn to right the wrong.

Memories dance like candlelight,
Illuminating dark of night.
Each note we sing, a prayer to share,
Binding our hearts, our silent care.

With tender grace, we honor those,
Who walked with us through joys and woes.
In every tear, a love bestowed,
In every word, a heavy load.

As echoes fade in quiet peace,
We find in sorrow, sweet release.
In every end, a new begin,
With every heart, we let love in.

## The Serene Weight of Goodbye

In the soft glow of fading light,
We gather 'round to hold what's right.
With heavy hearts and whispered sighs,
We share the burden of goodbyes.

Yet in this weight, a grace unfolds,
A testament that love upholds.
Each farewell whispers hope anew,
In parting ways, we find what's true.

Through tender hands, we pass the time,
In laughter shared, our hearts do climb.
For every soul, a path to find,
In gentle moments, love confined.

As we release what once was near,
We plant the seeds of future cheer.
In every tear that falls from eyes,
We breathe in strength, for love won't die.

## **The Sacred Art of Letting Go**

In the silence, whispers fade,
Each moment holds a sacred thread,
Release the bonds that tightly weigh,
For peace emerges where hearts tread.

Tears may fall like gentle rain,
Yet in their flow, the soul finds light,
Letting go, we embrace the pain,
Finding strength in letting night.

Surrender burdens to the sky,
Trust the path that lies ahead,
The sacred art in every sigh,
Is finding solace in what's shed.

From ashes rise a clearer mind,
A phoenix born from pain's embrace,
In the letting, joy we find,
In open arms, we find our place.

So here we stand in tender grace,
With hearts aligned to let love flow,
In every ending, see His face,
The sacred art of letting go.

## **Threads of Eternity Unraveled**

In the loom of time, we weave,
Threads of fate so tightly spun,
Each knot a lesson to believe,
In the weaver, we are one.

Patterns change with each new day,
Frayed edges speak of love and loss,
In every twist, a chance to pray,
Embracing fate, we bear the cross.

The tapestry reveals a grace,
Subtle hues of joy and sorrow,
Each thread a step in life's embrace,
Facing dawn beyond tomorrow.

As colors blend, we understand,
The sacred ties that bind us true,
In every heart, a guiding hand,
Threads of love, in me and you.

Reaching out, we grasp our fate,
With faith that leads us past the pain,
Threads of eternity correlate,
In the unravelling, we remain.

## The Garden of Forgotten Goodbyes

In shadows cast by yesterday,
Where whispers linger in the air,
The garden blooms in soft decay,
A place where hearts once laid bare.

Petals drift like fallen dreams,
Remembered in the gentle breeze,
Each goodbye, a silent scream,
Yet teaches love's eternal ease.

Among the roots of sacred ground,
Lies the essence of our trust,
In every loss, a joy profound,
For in the soil, we leave the dust.

New seeds of hope will take their flight,
As the sun breaks through the grey,
Goodbyes may fade into the night,
Yet love's refrain will always stay.

So tend the garden with the heart,
Embrace the beauty in the tear,
For hidden gifts, from pain, impart,
The garden blooms, forever dear.

## Celestial Lessons in Farewells

When stars align, we bid adieu,
In every parting, wisdom glows,
Each farewell holds a lesson true,
In darkness, light of love still flows.

The heavens dance in tranquil grace,
As comets carve a fleeting trail,
In gentle breath, each time and place,
Whispers of loss, yet love prevails.

Celestial truths are softly spun,
In the threads of cosmic time,
With every end, a new begun,
In unity, our spirits climb.

From shadows deep, the soul ascends,
In the embrace of night, we learn,
That every chapter gently bends,
To shape our hearts as candles burn.

So when the stars begin to fade,
And farewells linger in the skies,
Remember love will never trade,
Celestial lessons in goodbyes.

## A Quieting of Hearts

In stillness, we find grace,
Where shadows gently trace.
A whisper through the night,
Guiding souls towards the light.

In silence, burdens ease,
Hearts gathered, love to seize.
With faith that holds us tight,
Awakening our sight.

Each moment, softly blessed,
In solitude, we rest.
The heaven's breath we feel,
Our wounds, they start to heal.

When storms of life do roar,
We stand on sacred shore.
In prayer, we find our peace,
A quiet joy's release.

With spirits intertwined,
In harmony, aligned.
Together, we will soar,
To realms forevermore.

## **Eternal Echoes of Farewell**

In twilight's gentle sigh,
We whisper soft goodbye.
With tears like falling stars,
The heart, it bears the scars.

Each echo of your name,
A flame that stays the same.
In memories, you dwell,
In dreams, we break the shell.

Though distance stands apart,
In every beating heart,
Your love, a guiding star,
Forever near, not far.

As seasons turn the page,
We honor grief and age.
In laughter and in tears,
Your spirit perseveres.

With every silent prayer,
We're wrapped in love's own care.
In time's unfurling grace,
We meet beyond this place.

## The Prayer Mat Stained with Tears

Upon the mat, I kneel,
In sorrow, I reveal.
Each tear, a tender plea,
A cry to set me free.

In shadows of the night,
I seek the sacred light.
With every heartfelt word,
A solace felt, unheard.

The fabric bears the weight,
Of grief and quiet fate.
Yet in this sacred space,
I find my strength, my grace.

With faith, I gather breath,
Embracing life and death.
The mat, a witness true,
To shadows long overdue.

In whispers, I relate,
My burdened soul's estate.
In prayer, we rise anew,
With hope forever true.

## The Halo of Moments Lost

In every fleeting day,
A halo fades away.
Moments like petals fall,
In silence, they enthrall.

Through laughter, joy, and pain,
In echoes, we remain.
Each glance, a brush with fate,
In time, we contemplate.

The beauty of goodbye,
In memories, we lie.
Like stars that choose to glow,
In darkness, love we sow.

With every cherished breath,
We find the dance of death.
Yet in the twilight's grace,
We hold the lost embrace.

A tapestry of dreams,
In shadowed, sacred themes.
Through all we've come to know,
The light will ever glow.

## Faithful Wings Across the Threshold

In shadows cast by heaven's light,
We stand as souls, prepared to fight.
With faithful wings, we rise above,
Embraced by grace, wrapped in love.

The whispers of the angels call,
Through trials we ascend, not fall.
Each step adorned with sacred trust,
In faith we journey, rise from dust.

A path of hope, illuminated,
Each prayer a rhythm, celebrated.
With hearts united, strong and free,
We find our peace, our destiny.

In moments hushed, we seek the way,
With light and love to guide the day.
Ever faithful, onward we soar,
To the threshold where we restore.

When evening falls, and stars ignite,
We gather strength in holy light.
With faithful wings, let spirit sing,
Together we shall rise, take wing.

## **Wisdom Wrapped in Silence**

In the stillness, truths unfold,
Beyond mere words, the heart is bold.
Wrapped in silence, we hear it clear,
Wisdom whispers to those who hear.

In quiet moments, souls align,
Transcending doubt, as stars entwine.
A gentle touch, a knowing glance,
In silence we find our sacred chance.

Nature speaks in sacred sighs,
In tranquil woods, where spirit flies.
Embrace the peace, let go of haste,
Wrap yourself in moments chaste.

In solemn prayer, our minds set free,
Awakening to divinity.
With every breath, a sacred hymn,
In silence, wisdom's light won't dim.

Listen close to the quiet breath,
In silence, we dance with life and death.
For in the hush, our souls ignite,
Wisdom wrapped in the purest light.

## The Graceful Arc of Farewell

In twilight's glow, we see the end,
A graceful arc, on which we depend.
With heavy hearts, and eyes aglow,
In whispers soft, we learn to let go.

Each memory held within our chest,
A journey shared, a sacred quest.
Through laughter bright and tear-stained night,
Goodbye becomes our fleeting flight.

As petals fall from blooms once bright,
We cherish moments, in soft twilight.
With gentle hands, we weave the past,
In love we find our shadows cast.

Though distance calls and pathways stray,
In every heart, the echoes stay.
The arc of farewell bends towards grace,
In every tear, a warm embrace.

So let us honor what we've known,
In letting go, new seeds are sown.
With grateful hearts, we bid adieu,
The grace of farewell, forever true.

## Prayerful Soliloquy of Parting

In hushed tones, I speak to Thee,
A prayerful heart, set gently free.
In moments fleeting, time does sway,
A soliloquy, I humbly pray.

Each word a bridge, a sacred thread,
In stillness linger, where spirits tread.
With every sigh, the heavens near,
A dance of love, a voice sincere.

The echoes of goodbye resound,
In tender spaces, softly found.
With gentle grace, I take my leave,
In prayerful whispers, I believe.

Though paths may part and journeys split,
In sacred bonds, we still commit.
With open hearts, we share this grace,
The prayerful soliloquy we embrace.

For in each farewell, a hope takes flight,
Through sacred words in darkest night.
So let us weave this tapestry,
In love and light, we shall be free.

## Reverence in Letting Go

In the silence we bow our heads,
As the spirit begins to rise.
Threads of love lovingly severed,
Union becomes sweet goodbyes.

With hearts aglow, we set it free,
Trusting the path beyond our sight.
Each tear is a gift, a memory,
In the dawn, the soul takes flight.

Whispers of peace fill the air,
As we honor the journey made.
In both joy and aching despair,
Reverence blooms, our fears allayed.

The essence lingers, love remains,
In every shadow, light shall grow.
For in every loss, love sustains,
A cherished bond, forever flow.

Letting go, yet holding tight,
To the grace that will emerge.
In this sacred dance of light,
The heart and spirit gently urge.

## In the Shadow of the Eternal

Beneath the vast, embracing skies,
We step with faith into the light.
Guided by whispers of the wise,
Finding peace within the night.

In shadows cast by love's embrace,
We learn to breathe, we learn to feel.
Eternal echoes find their place,
As truth unfolds, our hearts will heal.

Every moment, both frail and bold,
Is a glimpse of the grand design.
Stories of ages, softly told,
In the sacred, eternal sign.

With gratitude for paths we tread,
We honor every soul we meet.
In the silence where hearts are led,
We weave the fabric, love complete.

In the shadow of what has been,
Hope rises like the morning's glow.
For in each loss, a precious skin,
A cycle richer as we grow.

## The Last Prayer of Farewell

As daylight wanes and stars ignite,
We gather close, our hearts entwined.
A final prayer, a soft goodnight,
In this love, our souls aligned.

Words of wisdom fill the air,
Each breath a whisper of goodbye.
In every longing, every care,
We send our love beyond the sky.

Holding hands, beneath the moon,
We share our dreams, our tender fears.
Through echoing silence, we attune,
In this moment, love perseveres.

For in the stillness, hope remains,
A promise flickers in the dark.
In every parting, love sustains,
Etched in time like a sacred mark.

The last prayer held in gentle grace,
A blessing for the road ahead.
In love's embrace, we find our place,
As life unfolds, our spirits spread.

## Shadows of Sacred Partings

In the dusk of cherished nights,
Where memories quietly sleep,
We honor the bond of sacred rites,
In the silence, love runs deep.

With heavy hearts, we gather near,
As the daylight fades away.
In every smile, we shed a tear,
In twilight's glow, we learn to stay.

The stories linger, softly spoken,
Of paths we traveled, joys and pain.
Though the ties may sometimes be broken,
In the heart, they still remain.

Shadows stretch but do not fade,
In love's embrace, we find our peace.
From fragile roots, our strength is laid,
In the dance of life, there's sweet release.

Together we walk this sacred ground,
In every parting, joy and sorrow.
Through shadows of love, we are found,
In tomorrow's light, we softly borrow.

## A Celestial Farewell

In the embrace of twilight's grace,
Angels whisper from their place,
Heaven's gate begins to part,
As light descends, we feel the heart.

With every tear, a prayer takes flight,
In memories held through the night,
Stars above with kindness gleam,
Guiding souls in a sacred dream.

The sky unfolds a tapestry,
Of love that lasts eternally,
In fleeting moments, we find peace,
A promise heard that will not cease.

With every step, the path is bright,
Through darkened valleys, we find light,
Emboldened by the holy word,
In silence, the truth is heard.

So wave goodbye to earthly ties,
While faith lifts us towards the skies,
Together we will rise again,
In unity, our spirits blend.

## Remnants of Reverence

In shadows cast by hallowed ground,
Echoes speak without a sound,
Whispers of those who came before,
Their love remains, forevermore.

The candles flicker, prayers take flight,
In softest glow of candlelight,
With every breath, a sacred bond,
In our hearts, their spirits respond.

Through sacred rites and songs of old,
The tales of wisdom are retold,
In the silence, their presence near,
A calming force, removing fear.

The fabric of time entwines us deep,
In the harvests of memories we keep,
Remnants of love that never fade,
In every promise solemnly made.

So lift our hearts, both brave and true,
With every prayer, we break anew,
In reverence, we find our way,
Knowing love is here to stay.

## **The Final Discourse of Love**

In the twilight of life's embrace,
Love unfolds with gentle grace,
Each heartbeat sings a sacred song,
In unity, where souls belong.

The final words, a soft refrain,
In every joy, in every pain,
We gather round, our hearts align,
In the healing hands of the divine.

With open arms, we share the light,
Through darkest hours, we find our sight,
In the love we tenderly weave,
A binding joy, a heart's reprieve.

The journey's end, a cherished start,
As love transcends the body's part,
In every smile, a memory stays,
Guiding us through endless days.

So fear not what the dawn will bring,
In love, we find our infinite spring,
Together bound in holy trust,
In every moment, love is a must.

## The Promise Beyond the Bye

When shadows fall and daylight fades,
A promise lives in twilight's shades,
With every sigh, a truth reveals,
In the heart, the spirit heals.

Though parting ways brings heavy hearts,
Love's journey flows, never departs,
Through every storm, through each goodbye,
A sacred bond will never die.

In the echoes of the past we learn,
With every light, a candle burns,
In grace, we trust what lies ahead,
In love, we find the words unsaid.

Across the realms, in unity's light,
Souls intertwine, a blessed sight,
The promise whispered, softly given,
In love, our spirits always driven.

So turn your face toward the dawn,
Embrace the love that carries on,
For in each tear, a joy will rise,
A promise lives beyond the skies.

## The Faith That Fades

In shadows where hope once gleamed,
The whispers of doubt now scheme.
Hearts tremble, their warmth grown cold,
A story of faith, silently told.

The prayers once lifted to the skies,
Dwindle like stars that fail to rise.
In silence we seek, yet we find,
The echoes of love left behind.

Through trials, our spirits wane,
Searching for light amidst the pain.
Yet in the twilight, grace remains,
A flicker of truth in heart's refrains.

The path may twist, the journey long,
But through the darkness, still we're strong.
In each falter, a chance to mend,
Faith's journey is not without end.

So hold the light, though it may fade,
For every prayer, a promise made.
In shadow's depth, a glimmer stays,
A spark of hope that gently prays.

## The Final Offering of Love

As twilight falls on weary day,
We gather near, in heartfelt sway.
Each whisper a soft, tender breath,
In this moment, we embrace death.

The hands once clasped in joy's delight,
Now release in the fading light.
With tears of sorrow, we bestow,
Our love, a gift, in quiet glow.

Each memory a soft echo sings,
Of laughter shared and the joy it brings.
A final offering, pure and true,
In every farewell, love breaks through.

With grace we stand, in silent prayer,
For those we hold in hearts laid bare.
Their journey continues beyond our sight,
In love's embrace, they take their flight.

So let us cherish, let us hold,
In every heart, their stories told.
For love remains, though parting sighs,
A timeless bond that never dies.

## **Heartstrings that Echo Beyond**

In the quiet of twilight's glow,
Heartstrings bind us, soft and slow.
Across the valleys, through the night,
We sing of love, a guiding light.

Each beat a tether, strong and clear,
A melody only the soul can hear.
With every breath, we reach for grace,
Finding solace in each embrace.

Though distance may seek to sever ties,
In whispered prayers, our spirit flies.
For love transcends both space and time,
In every heart, it finds its rhyme.

So when the stars begin to weep,
And memories fade into the deep,
Remember this truth from above,
Our heartstrings echo with endless love.

We gather strength from those who've gone,
Their light, a lantern, guiding on.
With every heartbeat, we stand as one,
In this sacred dance, our souls undone.

## The Communion of Farewells

In the circle of souls, we gather near,
To share our stories, to shed a tear.
With hearts unveiled, we stand as kin,
In the communion where love begins.

Each word a thread that weaves our fate,
Binding us close, never too late.
In every farewell, a promise made,
In the tapestry of love, we're laid.

With hands outstretched, we face the night,
Embracing shadows, seeking light.
For in this moment, we understand,
Together we rise, together we stand.

Though paths diverge and bodies tire,
The spark of love shall never expire.
In every parting, a sweet refrain,
A melody born of joy and pain.

So let us cherish each sacred breath,
In the communion that transcends death.
For every goodbye, a love endowed,
In heaven's grace, we're forever vowed.

## The Shimmering Path to Release

In the stillness, spirits soar high,
Whispers of grace, a guiding sigh.
In shadows of doubt, light will unfold,
As the heart learns to be bold.

Through trials faced, the soul will mend,
With faith as armor, the journey transcends.
Each step a blessing, each moment divine,
Releasing the burdens, a chance to align.

Beneath the stars where the heavens gleam,
Prayerful echoes, a sacred dream.
With open arms, we greet the dawn,
On this shimmering path, we are reborn.

In laughter and tears, the love we share,
Connects the threads of a cosmic prayer.
As we tread softly on this earth,
We find in release our truest worth.

With each heartbeat, a rhythm so sweet,
In the tapestry of life, our paths meet.
Together we wander, never alone,
On this shimmering path, love's light is shown.

## Holy Closure in Love's Embrace

In the still of night, love does whisper,
Softening hearts, as shadows flicker.
Within the warmth of a gentle touch,
We find our solace, we know so much.

With every gaze, a bond is formed,
Two souls entwined, beautifully warmed.
In the sacred silence, promises bloom,
In this holy closure, we find our room.

With every heartbeat, eternity flows,
In love's embrace, the spirit glows.
Together we dance in soft moonlight,
With passion ignited, the world feels right.

In laughter shared, and tears we heed,
Love's language spoken, fulfilling our need.
As we journey forth, hand in hand,
In this holy closure, we firmly stand.

With a whisper of faith, hearts become whole,
Wrapped in the light, we nourish the soul.
Forever entwined, our spirits rise,
In love's embrace, we touch the skies.

# Rituals of the Heart Unyielding

In the quiet dawn, soft notes appear,
Rituals of love, we hold so dear.
With open hearts, we gather near,
Together in faith, casting out fear.

In whispers sacred, our stories blend,
With every heartbeat, our spirits mend.
Through sacred rites, we lift the veil,
In meditation's grace, we will not fail.

With candles lit, our hopes ignite,
Guiding us through the longest night.
In every promise, a bond we weave,
In rituals of love, we truly believe.

With hands clasped tight, we journey forth,
In unity found, we measure our worth.
Through trials and triumphs, our path we chart,
In the sacred stillness, rituals start.

With every breath, we honor the past,
In the heart's embrace, we are steadfast.
Together we stand, through joy and pain,
In rituals of the heart, love will reign.

## The Quietude After the Storm

In the chaos, the tempest raged,
But in the stillness, we are engaged.
With each raindrop, a lesson falls,
In the quietude, the spirit calls.

As clouds disperse, the sun breaks through,
A gentle reminder of love so true.
In moments of calm, our hearts unwind,
After the storm, peace is enshrined.

With whispers soft, the winds embrace,
Healing the wounds, restoring grace.
For in the aftermath, the soul will bloom,
In the quietude, find room for the loom.

From turbulence born, new life shall rise,
In the silence, we hear the wise cries.
In reflection deep, wisdom is sown,
In the quietude after storms, we've grown.

With gratitude held, we stand anew,
In the warmth of the sunlight, a radiant view.
As the world awakens, we carry the light,
In the quietude found, everything feels right.

## Whispers of Farewell

In silence we gather, as day turns to night,
A soft breeze whispers, guiding the light.
With hearts heavy laden, we offer our prayers,
In the stillness of spirit, our love always shares.

Memories linger, like stars in the sky,
Each twinkle a blessing, a soft breath, a sigh.
Though paths may diverge, our souls intertwine,
In the garden of faith, forever you shine.

Farewell is a journey, not an end to the road,
In the tapestry woven, we carry the load.
With reverence we honor, the life that you led,
In the echoes of laughter, your spirit is wed.

Embrace the horizon, where sunlight will fall,
In the arms of the heavens, we answer the call.
For love knows no boundaries, nor distance can sever,
In the whispers of farewell, we find we are forever.

## Sacred Shadows Departing

In twilight's embrace, sacred shadows we trace,
The journey of souls, in a heavenly place.
Each heart that has wandered, returns to the light,
In the warmth of the Spirit, fading into the night.

With gratitude we gather, memories to share,
In the silence of sorrow, feel love everywhere.
Through tears that we shed, like raindrops they fall,
Each one a reminder of the grace that we call.

As angels surround us in divine, pure song,
They guide us with comfort, where we all belong.
With hands intertwined, we stand 'neath the stars,
In the glow of remembrance, we heal all the scars.

So bid not farewell, see it as a start,
In the circle of life, you are always a part.
In sacred shadows departing, we rise from the floor,
With hearts wide open, we embrace evermore.

## The Final Embrace of Grace

The final embrace, like a gentle caress,
In the arms of the heavens, we find our rest.
With sighs of the weary, we lay down our fears,
In the comfort of faith, we gather our tears.

With each passing moment, a story unfolds,
In the tapestry woven, our destiny molds.
Through joy and through sorrow, we've walked hand in hand,
Now we journey together to a far distant land.

The light softly beckons, sweet whispers of peace,
In the dance of the stars, our worries release.
As we treasure the blessings, the love that we knew,
In that final embrace, we are born anew.

So let not your heart be heavy with loss,
For grace is a compass, it guides us across.
In the sacredness found in the depths of our souls,
In the final embrace, forever we're whole.

## **Echoes of the Departed Soul**

In quiet reflection, we hear the soft call,
The echoes of voices that linger for all.
Each heartbeat a memory, a sigh of the past,
In the whispers of time, love's shadows are cast.

Through valleys of yearning, and mountains of peace,
The journey continues, may burdens release.
With eyes closed in reverence, we listen, we know,
In the echoes of the departed, true wisdom will flow.

With every remembrance, a lesson we gain,
In the tapestry woven, both joy and the pain.
For every farewell carries love's sacred hue,
In the echoes of souls, forever true.

As sunlight cuts through the most shadowed of days,
We celebrate life in all myriad ways.
So honor the departed, in heart and in mind,
For in echoes of their love, we are forever entwined.

## **Heavenly Lessons in Release**

In the stillness, whispers flow,
Teachings from skies above bestow.
Each burden shed, a gift of grace,
In surrender, we find our place.

With every tear that falls like rain,
Leaving behind the depth of pain.
With hearts awakened, spirits rise,
Through the shadows, we seek the skies.

Wisdom comes in quiet song,
Lessons learned where we belong.
In the night, the stars ignite,
Guiding souls to find their light.

Cleansing rivers cross our way,
In release, we learn to sway.
The weight of life, a fleeting breath,
In letting go, we find ourselves.

Embrace the dawn, a brand new start,
With open hands, we share our heart.
In heavenly lessons, we can see,
The love that sets our spirits free.

## **Celestial Comfort in Farewell**

Underneath the silver moon,
We gather soft, to sing a tune.
In every heartbeat, love will dwell,
With warmth that casts away the spell.

Memories like petals fall,
Each story shared, a sacred call.
In whispered words and gentle sighs,
Celestial comfort in goodbyes.

Though parting brings a thread of pain,
In each embrace, a soft refrain.
May hope arise with morning's light,
In every shadow, find the bright.

With angels near, we stand as one,
Cocooned in love, our spirits run.
Farewell is but a bridge we cross,
In every ending, find the gloss.

So let our hearts be filled with grace,
As we bid forth to that new place.
In celestial comfort, we shall find,
The bonds of love that intertwine.

## **The Prayer of Parting Hearts**

In silence sweet, we softly pray,
For hearts entwined to find their way.
Though time may pull our hands apart,
Love's echo lingers in the heart.

With every parting, blessings flow,
In distant lands, our spirits grow.
Through trials faced and joys we share,
In prayerful thought, we are laid bare.

May peace descend on weary souls,
As we embrace our distant goals.
In every journey, strength will shine,
Connected still, through love divine.

With every breath a whispered wish,
To hold you close, where souls can swish.
Though we depart, the thread remains,
In prayerful bonds, no heart complains.

As the stars speak from above,
We gather strength in faith and love.
So till we meet in skies anew,
This prayer shall guide my heart to you.

## Anointment of the Last Breath

At the edge of the earthly shore,
Awaits the grace of evermore.
With gentle hands, the veil we part,
Anointment flows within the heart.

As daylight fades and shadows creep,
In sacred silence, we find deep.
The final breath, a whisper sweet,
Carries love to where we meet.

With sacred oils, the spirit lifts,
In cherished moments, love sifts.
Through weary eyes, the light shines clear,
Embracing all we hold so dear.

Though death may come with subtle tread,
In every heart, love's not dead.
Anointment gives a holy grace,
In the passage to that blessed place.

So fear not the journey you must take,
For in our hearts, love will awake.
In every breath, a tender trace,
Anointment of eternal space.

## Embracing the Silent Benediction

In the stillness, hearts unite,
Whispers of grace fill the night.
Hands raised high, souls in prayer,
Finding peace in the silent air.

Mountains echo with the sound,
Of love's embrace, all around.
In reverence, we bend our knee,
To the whispers that set us free.

Each breath a blessing, soft and sweet,
In the quiet, our spirits meet.
Stars above, a guiding light,
Leading us through the endless night.

With each moment, we draw near,
The silent benedictions here.
Faith unfurls like petals bright,
In the dawn of sacred light.

Embracing all that is divine,
We find our souls begin to shine.
With every echo, we believe,
In the love that won't deceive.

## The Altar of Eternal Goodbyes

At the altar, shadows weep,
Promises made, a love to keep.
Words linger, softly entwined,
In the echoes, souls aligned.

Each farewell, a sacred mark,
Illuminated by the spark.
Through the veil, we hold on tight,
To the memories, pure and bright.

Candles flicker, spirits soar,
In this space, we are much more.
Hearts entwined in a gentle sway,
In the light, we find our way.

With every tear, a prayer is said,
For those departed, love is spread.
The altar stands with grace profound,
In the silence, love is found.

Though goodbyes echo in our hearts,
New journeys begin as old depart.
In the dusk, where shadows lie,
We find hope in the endless sky.

## Echoes in the Chamber of Departure

In the chamber where echoes dwell,
Silent stories weave their spell.
Whispers of those who passed this way,
In the twilight, they gently sway.

Voices linger, soft and clear,
Each farewell a song sincere.
Memories dance in the fading light,
Guiding souls into the night.

Hearts remember, even when lost,
In the stillness, we count the cost.
Every moment, a sacred gift,
In love's embrace, our spirits lift.

Farewell is but a fleeting breath,
In the cycle, we witness death.
Yet life continues, unbroken flow,
In the echoes, love will grow.

At the chamber's door we stand,
Holding tightly to love's command.
Though they leave, their spirits stay,
In our hearts, they find their way.

## A Soul's Journey Beyond the Veil

In the hush of twilight's grace,
A soul takes flight, finds its place.
Through the veil, it softly glides,
In the light, forever abides.

With every step, a story told,
Of love and warmth, of hearts so bold.
Retracing paths where shadows fell,
A celestial dance, all is well.

As the stars align in the vast deep,
The soul awakens from its sleep.
In the embrace of the divine,
Each note a song, each breath a sign.

Beyond the veil, no fear remains,
In the light, no soul complains.
A journey endless, pure and bright,
Guided by eternal light.

At the horizon, where dreams arise,
The soul rejoices, never dies.
In the divine, all love unveiled,
A sacred truth, forever hailed.

# From Ashes to Eternity

From ashes we rise, in faith reborn,
Through trials of fire, hearts are worn.
A promise of light, in shadows we tread,
Guided by grace, our spirits are fed.

In whispers of hope, love's gentle calls,
Transcending the veil, where each soul falls.
The journey unfolds, with every breath,
In the arms of the divine, we conquer death.

Through pain and despair, we seek the dawn,
In unity strong, our fears are gone.
Eternity waits, in the arms of the light,
With faith as our shield, we embrace the night.

Together we rise, as one we stand,
In the tapestry woven, by a sacred hand.
From ashes to glory, our stories are spun,
In the heart of the Maker, we are all one.

## **Carried on Wings of Goodbye**

In the still of the night, softly we part,
With whispers of love, deep in the heart.
Carried on wings, our souls take flight,
To realms of the blessed, in eternal light.

Through tears and laughter, memories stay,
In the book of our lives, they gently lay.
Each moment cherished, each promise held,
In faith we find strength, though love may be quelled.

From shadows we rise, together we soar,
Bound by our spirits, forevermore.
With every goodbye, a new journey starts,
In the silence of prayer, we heal aching hearts.

Though distance may stretch, love knows no end,
In the fabric of time, we eternally mend.
Carried on wings, we celebrate grace,
A sacred farewell, in the warmest embrace.

## **The Sacred Chorus of Departures**

In twilight's embrace, we gather near,
With voices uplifted, in love we steer.
A chorus resounds, as hearts intertwine,
In sacred departures, our spirits align.

Each soul a note, in the symphony divine,
Harmonies echo, through ages they shine.
In moments of loss, we find our way,
With prayers as our guide, we welcome the day.

Through mountains and valleys, our journey is blessed,
In leaving behind, we find peace and rest.
The ties that bind us, in faith we hold true,
In the sacred chorus, we sing anew.

Every departure, a promise to keep,
In the whisper of love, our memories seep.
In the heart of the journey, we find our light,
A sacred connection, in day and in night.

## **Candles Flickering in Twilight**

In twilight's soft glow, candles burn bright,
Their flames dance gently, dispelling the night.
Each flicker a prayer, a wish set free,
In the sacred stillness, our spirits agree.

With memories cherished, we gather as one,
A circle of warmth, as day turns to sun.
Through trials and joy, we hold each other tight,
In the language of love, we find our sight.

These candles, our hopes, in shadows they play,
Illuminating paths, guiding our way.
With every small flame, a promise is made,
In the tapestry woven, our fears start to fade.

As twilight gives way to the stars above,
We remember the light, we remember the love.
In the sacred twilight, our spirits take flight,
As candles flicker softly, we welcome the night.

## Remnants of a Holy Parting

In twilight's glow, we bid adieu,
With whispered prayers, our spirits flew.
The wounds of love, they slowly heal,
In sacred silence, truths reveal.

Each gaze a promise, each tear a spark,
Guiding us through the fading dark.
Memories linger like incense sweet,
In heart's embrace, our souls shall meet.

Heaven's breath upon our faces,
In parting grace, the soul embraces.
An echo faint of what once was,
In every heartbeat, still the cause.

A journey long, yet divine and vast,
The love we shared shall ever last.
Through veils of sorrow, joy transcends,
In every ending, a life ascends.

We walk the path, though torn apart,
With faith as guide, we find the heart.
For in the distance, light does gleam,
The remnants whisper of a dream.

## Pilgrimage to Letting Go

A sacred road beneath our feet,
With every step, release feels sweet.
The burdens carried, we lay down,
In humble trust, we lose the crown.

The mountains echo our soft cries,
As blessings rain from starlit skies.
With open hands, we let it flow,
Into the stillness, peace will grow.

In every heartbeat, we depart,
From days long past, we guard the heart.
A pilgrimage through pain and grace,
In every scar, a holy trace.

The shadows dance as light appears,
Transforming sorrows into cheers.
With faith as compass, hope as guide,
In letting go, love shall abide.

The temple of the soul now free,
Unfettered joy, a jubilee.
In whispers soft, the angels sing,
The journey starts as we take wing.

## Seraphic Echoes in Silence

In silent prayer, the spirits hear,
The echo of a heart so dear.
The stillness speaks of sacred truths,
Where light breaks forth and darkness soothes.

Beneath the stars, we find our peace,
In moments fleeting, love won't cease.
Each breath a psalm, each sigh a song,
In seraphic whispers, we belong.

Through every trial, our faith refined,
In calm repose, divine aligned.
Expectations fade, the soul takes flight,
In silent echoes, we find the light.

As stillness reigns, we learn to see,
The beauty found in mystery.
A tapestry of hope is spun,
In sacred stillness, we are one.

In quiet moments, grace abounds,
With every heartbeat, love surrounds.
The echoes linger, soft and clear,
In silence shared, the Divine is near.

## The Divine Art of Departure

In solemn grace, we learn to part,
Fingers unthread, yet bound by heart.
The lessons learned, like chiseled stone,
In every parting, seeds are sown.

The art of leaving, tenderly taught,
In whispered breezes, wisdom caught.
Each farewell etched in sacred lore,
A step toward what lies evermore.

With every tear, a blessing flows,
Through open doors, the spirit grows.
In sacred moments, love shall bloom,
From ashes rise, dispelling gloom.

In letting go, we find our wings,
A flight of grace as the spirit sings.
The journey forward, though it seems dire,
Through sacred art, we lift higher.

In parting light, our souls entwine,
A testament to love divine.
For every ending finds a start,
In the divine art of the heart.

# Embracing the Solitary Journey

In the stillness of the night,
Whispers guide the wandering soul.
Each step unfolds new light,
Forging paths to make us whole.

Alone, yet never forsaken,
In solitude, we find our grace.
The heart, though weary and shaken,
Discovers strength in quiet space.

Through valleys deep and shadows long,
Faith is the compass in the dark.
Melodies of the spirit's song,
Echo softly, leaving a mark.

With every breath, a prayer ascends,
Sublime purpose in the unseen.
The journey's end, where love transcends,
A tapestry of hope, serene.

So let us walk, though paths be rough,
In silence, we shall find our way.
For in the soul, the journey's tough,
Yet sacred light guides through the gray.

Embrace the night, embrace the dawn,
For in solitude, we rise anew.
The path is ours, though alone,
In the heart, the journey's true.

# The Ritual of Letting Go

In the soft glow of evening's hue,
We gather all the burdens near.
With open hands, we start anew,
Releasing all that brings us fear.

A whispered prayer escapes the tongue,
As shadows dance along the ground.
We cast away what once was sung,
In the sacred air, we're unbound.

The heart, a vessel, filled to brim,
With memories that weigh like stone.
Yet in this moment, the light grows dim,
And freedom calls us to atone.

With gratitude, we cherish past,
Each lesson learned a stepping stone.
In letting go, the soul is cast,
To higher realms, no longer lone.

So breathe in deep, the freshened air,
In release, the spirit soars high.
For in this breath, we meet the rare,
The grace of change, where we comply.

The ritual done, we stand anew,
In silence, we embrace the flow.
The heart now open, pure, and true,
In letting go, our spirits grow.

## **Between the Heartbeats of Absence**

In the silence, absence speaks,
Whispers echo through the void.
Each heartbeat aches, yet gently seeks,
The love that time has not destroyed.

Moments linger, stretched like sighs,
Hope flickers like a distant star.
In shadows cast by gentle lies,
We find our healing from afar.

Through tears that glisten, truth reveals,
The weight of longing keeps us near.
Between each heartbeat, solace feels,
The fragile dance of love's sincere.

Yet in this space of quiet grace,
We learn the art of holding on.
Though absence may our dreams efface,
The heart knows light beyond the dawn.

So let us dwell in these sweet sighs,
For in the stillness, peace bestows.
Between the heartbeats, love defies,
The distance cast, yet never goes.

In absence, sacred bonds remain,
A tapestry of hope affirmed.
So breathe, for love transcends the pain,
In heartbeats true, the soul is burned.

## The Sacred Space of Silence

In silence deep, where spirits dwell,
The whispers of the universe hum.
In quietude, we hear the bell,
That calls us forth, a sacred drum.

Moments pause, eternity breathes,
As shadows fade and light breaks through.
In stillness, our wandering weaves,
A tapestry of all that's true.

The heart expands, a vessel wide,
To hold the echoes of the past.
In silence, we choose not to hide,
Finding strength in what will last.

Beneath the stars, a tranquil space,
Where thoughts like rivers gently flow.
In silence, we embrace the grace,
That love bestowed when hearts let go.

So gather here, in sacred calm,
Where words dissolve and hearts align.
In silence, we discover balm,
The sacred art of love divine.

And as the night whispers her song,
We find our stillness, ever near.
In this space where we belong,
The sacred silence draws us clear.

## **Divine Threads Unraveling**

In the quiet hum of prayer,
Faith intertwines with despair.
Each moment, a tapestry sewn,
In the hands of grace, we've grown.

Whispers of love in the night,
Guiding lost souls to the light.
Divine designs weave through time,
Echoing notes of the sublime.

Questions rise like smoke in air,
Yet in stillness, we find care.
Lessons learned in gentle hands,
In surrender, our heart expands.

With each thread that gently breaks,
A new path of wisdom wakes.
Suffering carves our spirit deep,
In faith's embrace, we truly leap.

Ribbons of hope tangle and twine,
In the hands of the Divine.
We walk beneath the heavens' gaze,
Awash in the Eternal's praise.

# Beneath the Stars We Bide

Beneath the stars, we find our fate,
In quiet moments, we await.
The whispers of the night reveal,
Unseen forces, soft and real.

Heaven's canvas spreads so wide,
A symphony in which we bide.
Faith like lighthouses arrive,
Guiding us to truly thrive.

Each twinkling star above us glows,
With stories of love that the heart knows.
In cosmic dance, we intertwine,
A glimpse of grace, a touch divine.

With every breath, we seek and soar,
In the stillness, we implore.
The universe sings a sacred song,
In each note, we find where we belong.

Through trials, our spirits take flight,
Beneath the stars, we seek the light.
Love surrounds us, ever near,
In the darkness, we cast off fear.

## An Attic of Memories Unbound

In the attic where shadows play,
Memories linger, refuse to sway.
Whispers of laughter, echoes of tears,
Carried through the passage of years.

Boxes of dreams, dusty with time,
Each trinket holds a tale sublime.
When twilight beckons, we recall,
The sacred moments, both great and small.

Love writes verses on heartstrings tight,
Guiding lost souls back to light.
In cherished relics, we find our peace,
From burdens of yesterdays, a release.

As we sift through fragments so dear,
A tapestry woven with joy and fear.
In every corner of this space,
We greet the past with a warm embrace.

Letting the echoes forge our way,
In remembrance, we choose to stay.
With open hearts, we step out free,
In the attic, our souls find glee.

# The Sacrament of Letting Go

In the stillness, where shadows dwell,
A sacrament of love we tell.
Releasing burdens, we find grace,
In surrender, we find our place.

Tides of sorrow ebb and flow,
Yet in this cycle, we learn to grow.
The weight of loss opens our eyes,
To the beauty in each goodbyes.

With clasped hands, we part the night,
In silence, we seek the light.
Trusting the path we cannot see,
In every ending, we're set free.

Memories blossom, fade away,
In letting go, we find our way.
Through love's embrace, we navigate,
To a future bright that awaits.

So raise your hearts and breathe in deep,
Harvest the lessons that life keeps.
In the sacrament, our souls align,
Letting go, we intertwine.

## Hearts Unbound in Sacred Trust

In shadows deep, we find our way,
With whispered prayers that softly sway.
In unity, we stand as one,
Our hearts unbound, till day is done.

With trust divine and spirits bold,
We share the love that can't be sold.
Together, we rise above our fears,
In sacred truth, we dry our tears.

Hear the call of grace so bright,
Guiding souls through endless night.
In every heart, a sacred flame,
Connected souls, in love's sweet name.

The journey long, yet filled with grace,
Each step we take, a holy space.
In faith we gather, side by side,
In hearts unbound, our hopes reside.

Let not the doubts of this world sway,
For love will guide us on our way.
With every breath, we sing and trust,
In sacred bonds, our hearts combust.

## A Quiet Reverie of Release

In silence deep, the spirit sighs,
A gentle peace beneath the skies.
We rest our thoughts, let worries cease,
In quiet reverie, find our peace.

Release the burdens we once bore,
As waves retreat upon the shore.
With every breath, we let it go,
Embracing calm, our spirits flow.

In nature's arms, we feel the grace,
A tender touch, a warm embrace.
In stillness found, our hearts are free,
A quiet gift of harmony.

As twilight falls, we close our eyes,
With whispered love that never dies.
In reverie, we soar above,
Bathed in the warmth of boundless love.

So let us wander, hand in hand,
Together dreaming, heart unplanned.
In moments still, we find our light,
A quiet reverie takes flight.

## **The Faithful Evening of Farewell**

At dusk we gather, hearts entwined,
In faithful bonds, our souls aligned.
The whispers soft, as shadows grow,
In evening's grace, we let love flow.

With tearful eyes, we greet the night,
A gentle end, yet souls in flight.
Through heartfelt words and silent prayers,
We carry forth, the love that cares.

Each moment shared, a treasure dear,
In farewells, there's joy and fear.
But in this evening's soft embrace,
Our spirits dance, our hearts find place.

As stars arise, the night unfolds,
With stories shared, our truth beholds.
Though paths diverge, our hearts remain,
In faithful bonds, we'll meet again.

So raise a glass to memories made,
In laughter bright, and heartache laid.
For in this night, we feel the grace,
Of faithful love, in every space.

# The Graced Departure

In morning light, we bid adieu,
With hearts aglow, in love so true.
The world awaits, our spirits soar,
In graced departure, we seek more.

With every step, a journey calls,
The path is bright as sunlight falls.
We walk together, hand in hand,
With hope that blooms in every land.

Though distance looms, we hold the flame,
In every heart, we feel the same.
A sacred bond that time can't sever,
In graced departure, we're forever.

With whispered prayers and kind goodbyes,
We carry forth, beneath the skies.
In faith we find, our way is clear,
In every heartbeat, love is near.

So let us venture, brave and bold,
With stories shared, our hearts unfold.
In graced departure, life begins,
Embracing joy, as love wins.

## The Hushed Altar of Farewells

In silence we gather, hearts entwined,
Beneath a sky woven, by love's design.
Each tear a whisper, each sigh a plea,
At this altar of memories, we set them free.

The candle's glow flickers, a dance of the divine,
Illuminating shadows where your spirit shines.
Your voice echoes softly, in the still of the night,
Guiding us gently, towards the eternal light.

A moment of stillness, a breath held tight,
In the embrace of our grief, we find sacred right.
Each heartbeat a promise, each thought a prayer,
Carrying your essence, forever we bear.

As petals lay down, upon sacred ground,
In nature's soft cradle, your solace is found.
With every farewell, our faith we renew,
In the hush of this altar, we honor you.

So let us remember, in laughter and tears,
The bond that transcends both sorrow and years.
With love as our beacon, we gather and stand,
In the hushed altar of farewells, hand in hand.

## Sacred Waves of Parting

Along the shore, where the oceans sweep,
The waves whisper secrets, our hearts to keep.
In the rhythm of tides, we find our way,
Sacred waves of parting, guiding the day.

The horizon stretches, where heaven meets earth,
In the depths of our souls, we cherish your worth.
Each crest a memoir, each trough a sigh,
In the embrace of the sea, we learn to let fly.

With each rising sun, new colors emerge,
Yet the echo of your laughter continues to surge.
The salt of our tears mingles with the sand,
In nature's vast arms, we learn to withstand.

Though miles may divide us, love holds us close,
In the whispering waves, that comforts and glows.
With faith in tomorrow, we rise and we stand,
Sacred waves of parting, forever unplanned.

So as we bid farewell, with the setting sun,
We carry your spirit, in every run.
In the depths of our hearts, you forever reside,
In these sacred waves, you shall never hide.

## **A Covenant with the Departed**

In shadows we linger, a pact forged in grace,
With those who have journeyed, to a distant place.
A covenant whispered, in silence we vow,
To hold their light steady, here and now.

The stars overhead, like candles at night,
Guide our wandering hearts toward eternal light.
In prayers and in memories, we carve your name,
In this sacred embrace, we feel no shame.

Each moment a treasure, each memory shared,
In the warmth of your spirit, we find that we cared.
For love is a bond that time cannot sever,
In this covenant with souls, forever and ever.

Through trials and triumphs, we carry you near,
In laughter and sorrow, your presence is clear.
So gather around, let our hearts intertwine,
In this sacred promise, your light we enshrine.

As dusk settles gently, with whispers of peace,
Our covenant remains, may our love never cease.
For in every moment, in every prayer,
The departed are with us, forever they share.

## The Abyss of Luminous Goodbyes

In the still of the night, where shadows depart,
We tread through the abyss, each carrying a heart.
With luminous goodbyes, we face the unknown,
In this sacred moment, we are never alone.

The stars illuminate paths, we've yet to reveal,
With whispers of love, our wounds begin to heal.
In every farewell, there's a spark divine,
A tether of hope, where our spirits align.

Through valleys of sorrow, we walk hand in hand,
In the warmth of remembrance, together we stand.
Each tear a testament, each smile a prayer,
In the abyss of goodbyes, we find love everywhere.

As dawn breaks anew, with colors so bright,
We carry their essence, into the light.
For every heart's passage, a story unfolds,
In the depths of these goodbyes, a truth to behold.

So let us journey onward, with love as our guide,
Through the abyss of goodbyes, they walk by our side.
In the luminous glow, their memory lives on,
In every whispered prayer, they are never gone.

## Guardians of the Departed

In shadows deep, they watch and guide,
The souls that wander, unconfined.
With tender hearts and hands of light,
They carry us through the endless night.

In whispered prayers, their voices rise,
Echoing love that never dies.
With every tear, a promise made,
In memory's glow, we'll never fade.

Through tempest's roar, their strength we feel,
A sacred bond that wounds can heal.
They walk beside, both near and far,
As steadfast as the evening star.

In sacred time, they softly tread,
On pathways where our dreams are led.
With every breath, they share our pain,
And guide us home to peace again.

In gratitude, we lift our song,
For guardians true, where we belong.
Our hearts entwined in love's embrace,
We find our strength in boundless grace.

## **In the Arms of the Divine**

Embraced by light, we are made whole,
In sacred arms, our weary souls.
With every breath, we feel the grace,
Of love that shines in every place.

In prayers whispered, hopes take flight,
As shadows dance in endless night.
The heart's devotion, pure and bright,
Connects us all, both day and night.

The trials faced become the art,
Of growing close, each beating heart.
In silence deep, we hear the voice,
Of the Divine, a gentle choice.

Through storms we walk, with faith our guide,
In every moment, side by side.
For in the depths of sorrow's call,
The arms of Love will catch our fall.

With every tear, a lesson learned,
In every hope, a passion burned.
With faith we rise, a soul's ascent,
In the arms of Love, forever content.

## The Spiritual Alchemy of Farewell

In parting's grasp, we find the gold,
A secret power to enfold.
Through loss we learn, through grief we grow,
In sacred transformation, love will flow.

Each farewell whispers of rebirth,
The soul's sweet journey upon this earth.
In darkened hours, a light appears,
Alchemical path forged through our tears.

With every sigh, a story ends,
Yet in that space, the spirit mends.
Transcendence blooms where shadows lay,
In love's embrace, we find our way.

The sacred dance of death and life,
In every joy, in every strife.
A tapestry woven, rich and bright,
In every heart, a guiding light.

In gratitude, we honor change,
For every soul, a path to range.
With each goodbye, a new hello,
In love's pure flame, we come to know.

## A Lament for What Remains

In quiet moments, whispers call,
The echoes of those we recall.
A tender ache, a heavy heart,
For memories cherished, yet torn apart.

Through veils of time, their laughter lingers,
In every thought, we feel their fingers.
With heavy eyes, we seek the light,
In shadows deep, we find our sight.

The heart remembers all that's lost,
In love's embrace, we bear the cost.
For every smile, a tear will fall,
In silent reverie, we hear their call.

Yet through the grief, hope gently stays,
In every dawn, we find our ways.
The spirits rise, they never part,
Their essence lives within our heart.

A lament sung, yet not in vain,
For love endures, through joy and pain.
In every memory, a sacred sign,
They dwell with us, in love's design.

## The Hallowed Ground of Goodbyes

In silence, we gather, hearts entwined,
With memories woven, love defined.
Each farewell whispered, a sacred note,
In the hallowed ground, our spirits float.

Tears like rivers, flowing free,
Reflecting the bond of you and me.
In every echo, a prayer we send,
Embracing the promise, we'll meet again.

The sun dips low, casting its glow,
Over those we've cherished, now gone below.
Yet in the shadows, their light remains,
Guiding our souls through joys and pains.

We stand united in this sacred space,
Finding comfort in love, a warm embrace.
For parting brings strength, though hearts do ache,
In the hallowed ground, no one forsakes.

As seasons change and time does flow,
We honor the paths that we both know.
In every heartbeat, their presence thrives,
In the hallowed ground, where memory survives.

## **Emptiness Filled with Grace**

In the stillness of night, a whisper calls,
A gentle reminder when sorrow falls.
For in the void, grace softly weaves,
A tapestry rich, though the heart grieves.

Every ache bears a lesson bright,
In shadows, the dawn brings forth light.
Through empty chambers, faith ignites,
Transforming despair into sacred rites.

With each breath, we learn to believe,
That emptiness holds what we can achieve.
For in the silence, His presence is near,
Filling the gaps with love sincere.

Among the ruins of dreams once held,
A seed of hope, divinely quelled.
From ashes burn strength reborn,
In the empty spaces, grace is sworn.

Though loneliness wraps its cold embrace,
In faith, we find our rightful place.
With hearts open wide, we choose to see,
The emptiness filled with grace, truly free.

## Psalms of the Departed Heart

In whispered psalms, the heart does sing,
Of souls departed on angel's wing.
Memories cherished, like stars that gleam,
In the dark of night, they softly dream.

With every tear, a story told,
Of love enduring, both brave and bold.
Each note a promise, forever to stay,
In the warmth of light that won't decay.

The heavens open, welcoming grace,
As the departed find their sacred space.
Their laughter echoes through time and space,
In the psalms of love, they leave a trace.

We gather together, with hearts aligned,
Honoring those whom we've left behind.
In every heartbeat, they are alive,
In psalms of the departed, we thrive.

For love is a bond that cannot break,
In God's embrace, our souls partake.
We sing their praises, the journey's start,
In the psalms we carry, forever in heart.

## Celestial Roads Diverged

Upon the roads where destinies meet,
Two paths emerged, the choice was sweet.
In faith, we journey, hand in hand,
With every step, as He had planned.

Yet time dims light, and paths may part,
In silence spoken, the heavy heart.
Though roads diverge, love does not cease,
In every prayer, we find our peace.

With gentle winds, we bid farewell,
To dreams once shared, in joy they swell.
In the distance, we hear the call,
Of celestial paths leading us all.

In the twilight glow, we seek the way,
Guided by stars that brightly sway.
Though journeys differ, we're never alone,
In the heart's compass, love is home.

So as we travel, though roads may diverge,
With faith as our anchor, we'll never surge.
Through every trial, we'll find the light,
Celestial roads, in love's true sight.

## Illuminated Paths of Remembrance

In the quiet whispers of the night,
Memories dance in soft, gentle light.
Each step taken on sacred ground,
Echoes of love in silence found.

Stars above, like candles aglow,
Guide our hearts through ebb and flow.
With each breath, a prayer we share,
Connected in spirit, beyond despair.

In the garden of time, we tread slow,
A tapestry woven, wisdom to sow.
The spirit of those who once were here,
Fills the void, calms every fear.

With kindness, our souls intertwine,
In radiant love, both yours and mine.
Illuminate paths where shadows creep,
In the gentle embrace, our memories keep.

Through trials and sorrows, we find grace,
In each other's eyes, a sacred place.
For in remembrance, we truly live,
In the love of the past, we always forgive.

## Sanctified Journey into the Unknown

Upon the horizon, a dawn so bright,
Whispers of promise invite our flight.
With faith as our compass, we boldly tread,
Into the realms where angels spread.

A journey unfolds, where shadows abide,
In the heart's solace, we shall confide.
Through uncharted waters, we sail with grace,
Hand in hand, in this sacred space.

Mountains rise and valleys bend,
Yet our spirits, unwavering, shall not end.
In the embrace of the great unknown,
We find the seeds of hope we've sown.

Each step a testament to love's embrace,
In the labyrinth of time, we find our place.
Through challenges faced, our spirits soar,
Ever onward, we seek evermore.

With the light of the divine shining bright,
Fear dissolves in the presence of light.
In the unknown, we shall thrive,
Guided by faith, forever alive.

## **The Light of What Was**

In the quiet of dusk, a shimmer glows,
Reflecting on moments, as the memory flows.
Upon sacred ground, time stands still,
Holding the echoes of the heart's will.

Stories of old dance through the night,
In the warmth of the past, we find our light.
In the tapestry woven with threads of gold,
The wisdom of ages silently unfolds.

Each tear shed is a testament bright,
To the love we've known, our guiding light.
From the ashes, new dreams arise,
In the illumination of countless skies.

Let us gather the fragments of yesteryear,
In the sanctuary of memory, hold them dear.
For in what was, we find our way,
Illuminated paths lead us each day.

Through the shadows of grief, we find peace,
In the legacy of love, we find release.
Together we rise, hearts intertwined,
In the light of what was, our souls aligned.

## Angels in the Moments Before

In the stillness, angels softly descend,
Cloaked in the whispers that love can send.
Their presence, a balm to the weary heart,
Gathering fragments when we drift apart.

With wings unfurled in the twilight air,
They gather each prayer, lay our burdens bare.
In the moments before, they stand near,
Gifting us solace, whispering cheer.

When shadows loom and doubt takes hold,
The promise of light within us unfolds.
Through the veil, they guide with grace,
Leading us onward, a sacred embrace.

In laughter and tears, they silently guide,
In every heartbeat, they're by our side.
With love's gentle touch, they cradle our pain,
In the moments before, hope's sweet refrain.

So let us remember, in trials we face,
Angels are with us, life's holy lace.
In the tapestry of moments, we know it's true,
In every heartbeat, they're watching us too.

# Candles of Memory in the Dark

In the stillness of night, we ignite,
Candles of memory, flickering light.
Whispers of loved ones, softly they call,
In shadows they linger, love conquers all.

With each gentle flame, a story unfolds,
Pictures of laughter, of hearts that are bold.
Embers of grace, burn bright through the tears,
Guiding our spirits to comfort our fears.

Each candle a prayer, each flicker a hope,
Binding our souls, we're learning to cope.
In the darkened hours, we stand hand in hand,
Together in silence, we make our last stand.

As time softly passes, the flames may grow dim,
Yet love, like the stars, will never grow thin.
In memory's garden, we bloom and we share,
Caring, we're lifted, on wings of a prayer.

So let the candles burn, a beacon divine,
For in every heartbeat, their light shall entwine.
In the depths of the night, our spirits will soar,
Through the candles of memory, forevermore.

## Through the Portal of Parting

In the silence of dusk, we pause and reflect,
Through portals of parting, our hearts connect.
With tears like raindrops, we stand side by side,
In the depths of sorrow, love will abide.

As the sun slowly sets, shadows grow long,
We gather our thoughts and sing our last song.
Each heartbeat a promise, each breath a release,
In the arms of the night, we find our peace.

Through pain of goodbyes, the spirit will rise,
In dreams of the night, love never dies.
With every good wish that sails on the breeze,
We cherish the moments, like leaves on the trees.

Memories linger like stars in the sky,
Through the portal of parting, we learn how to fly.
As dawn gently breaks, a new path appears,
In the light of our love, we conquer our fears.

Though the journey feels heavy, and miles stretch ahead,
Our hearts are united, through paths that we tread.
In the whispers of time, we find our way clear,
Through the portal of parting, we hold what is dear.

## The Wordless Departure

In a moment of silence, the world stands still,
The wordless departure, hearts begin to fill.
No need for goodbyes, no fear of the end,
In the echoes of love, our souls will transcend.

With eyes full of longing, we share one last glance,
In the rhythm of fate, we dance our last dance.
No language required, just knowing and grace,
In the tapestry woven, we find our place.

As spirits take flight, like birds in the breeze,
The wordless departure sets our hearts at ease.
In each sacred moment, the past will not fade,
Through whispers of love, our memories cascade.

In the stars that guide us, in the moon's gentle sway,
The wordless departure shows us the way.
For though we are parted, we're never alone,
In the vastness of love, we've forever grown.

So let the silence speak, let the stillness be loud,
In the wordless departure, we stand ever proud.
Together in spirit, forever entwined,
In the depths of our hearts, a love undefined.

## The Sermon on Letting Go

In the chapel of life, we gather to learn,
The sermon on letting go, our hearts gently turn.
With each whispered word, we seek to release,
The burdens we carry, the call for peace.

Like leaves in the fall, we must learn to fall,
To thrive in the change, to heed the heart's call.
In the warmth of acceptance, we find our true ground,
Embracing the beauty that love has unbound.

Forgiveness is power, a gift we must share,
In letting go softly, we lighten our care.
In the cycle of seasons, life teaches us well,
Through letting go's grace, we find our own swell.

As the dawn breaks anew, let your heart sing,
The sermon on letting go teaches us wing.
For every goodbye opens a doorway to grace,
In the arms of acceptance, we find our true place.

So hoist up your sails, let the winds take you far,
In the sermon on letting go, we shine like a star.
With faith as our compass, we rise and we flow,
In the journey of love, we continue to grow.

# Beneath the Veil of Departure

In silent prayer we gather near,
Where memories linger, whispers clear.
Beneath the veil, our hearts entwine,
With every tear, the light will shine.

The paths we walk may twist and sway,
Yet faith will guide us on our way.
Transcending time, no bond can sever,
In love's embrace, we'll part forever.

Though shadows fall and clouds may rise,
We seek the grace beyond the skies.
In holy light, we'll find our place,
We'll hold each other in God's grace.

With every breath, the promise flows,
Of destinies that love bestows.
Through trials faced and joys we share,
In faith and hope, we find our prayer.

As we depart, we know as one,
Our souls will shine like the morning sun.
In sacred trust, we let love lead,
Beneath the veil, we're truly freed.

# The Covenant of Distant Love

Across the miles, the heavens sing,
Of promises that love can bring.
In each soft prayer, our spirits meet,
With tender grace, our hearts repeat.

This covenant, a sacred bond,
In every moment, we respond.
Though distance keeps our bodies far,
Our love remains a shining star.

In twilight's hue, we find our peace,
As hope and faith will never cease.
With every thought, we bridge the space,
In joyful praise, we seek His grace.

Through starlit nights and sunlit days,
In heart and soul, our love displays.
A journey shared, though paths are wide,
In spirit's light, we walk beside.

Let not the trials shake our will,
For love endures, our dreams fulfill.
In prayerful whispers, we unite,
This distant love shines ever bright.

## **Embracing the Divine Divide**

In spaces vast, where silence reigns,
We find the peace amidst our pains.
Embracing all, both grace and strife,
The divine thread weaves through our life.

Though we may stand on either shore,
In faith's embrace, we are much more.
A tapestry of love so grand,
United hearts, though not at hand.

In faith we rise, in love we stand,
Holding hope like grains of sand.
Through trials faced, we learn to see,
The beauty in what's meant to be.

Each challenge met with open heart,
Though physical, we're never apart.
In whispered prayers, our souls ignite,
Embracing all with love's pure light.

So let the divide draw us near,
In every moment, love is here.
With faith as guide and love's strong hand,
We'll walk together, always stand.

## The Cherubic Goodbye

In innocence, the angels sigh,
With tearful eyes, they bid goodbye.
In soft embrace, our spirits soar,
A cherubic light, forevermore.

Through golden gates and skies of blue,
The echoes of our love ring true.
In heavenly realms, we take our flight,
With joyous hearts, we chase the light.

In every tear, a memory gleams,
Each moment shared, fulfilling dreams.
As we unite in sacred space,
We hold the promise of His grace.

Though journeys part, our loves remain,
In every heartbeat, joy or pain.
Together still, our souls entwined,
In cherubic bliss, our paths aligned.

So let us not mourn this day,
For love transcends in every way.
In purest light, we find our way,
Cherubic hearts, forever stay.

## **Divine Epiphanies at Twilight**

In the hush of evening's glow,
Whispers of grace begin to flow.
Stars weave tales of faith and light,
Guiding souls through dark of night.

Heaven's canvas, painted bright,
Each stroke a promise, pure and right.
In moments still, divinity speaks,
Strengthening the hearts of the meek.

As shadows stretch, the spirit soars,
Revealing pathways to ancient shores.
In every breath, in every sigh,
The sacred calls—do not deny.

With open hearts, we seek the sign,
In twilight's arms, the love divine.
Embracing what the heavens share,
Transcendence rises through the air.

A gentle breeze, the angels sing,
Awakening the hopes we bring.
In faith, we find our place to stand,
As twilight bids us to expand.

## Ascending Through the Veils of Parting

Through the shadows, softly tread,
Where the sacred whispers spread.
Veils of separation drop away,
Revealing truths in bright array.

With each step, the spirit dances,
In the light, it swiftly prances.
Echoes of love pull us near,
In the face of every fear.

Tears of sorrow, now transformed,
In sacred spaces, hearts are warmed.
Guided by a gentle hand,
We find the strength to understand.

Each farewell, a door that swings,
To a world where hope still clings.
As we rise beyond the pain,
The promise of love will remain.

Through the veils, our souls will meet,
In the core of love, complete.
Ascend with faith, our prayers will soar,
Together forever, evermore.

# The Blessings We Leave Behind

In the footprints made on earth,
Lie the echoes of our worth.
Kindness spreads like morning light,
A ripple born from love's delight.

Each smile shared, a silent aid,
A testament to prayers laid.
Through our deeds, the spirit flies,
Lifting hearts towards the skies.

What we give is not in vain,
For blessings flow in joy and pain.
In love's embrace, we find our place,
Leaving traces of endless grace.

While mortal ties may come undone,
Heaven's love forever spun.
The seeds we've sown will thrive anew,
In the hearts we touched, it fingers through.

As we part, let love remain,
Echoing soft through joy and pain.
The blessings we leave will always bind,
A tapestry of hearts aligned.

## Tears of an Angel's Farewell

In the stillness, shadows weep,
An angel's heart begins to seep.
With every tear, a story flows,
Of love that's lost yet still bestows.

Wings that whisper soft goodbyes,
In the twilight, a spirit flies.
Though parting brings a heavy sigh,
In tears, the promise will not die.

Every droplet holds a prayer,
For moments cherished, always there.
In pain, we find the strength to heal,
Through love, the spirit learns to feel.

As twilight fades, the stars ignite,
Guiding souls in the silent night.
When angels weep, they weave a thread,
Connecting heart to heart, though dead.

So we gather the fallen light,
And hold it close through darkest night.
In tears of sorrow, joy concealed,
In an angel's farewell, love revealed.

## **A Hymn for Those We Release**

In quietude we gather round,
With hearts entwined, love profound.
We honor souls that drift away,
In gentle whispers, here we pray.

From earthly bonds, they now take flight,
Into the arms of sacred light.
Their laughter lingers, memories dear,
In every tear, they too are near.

Let time reshape the way we grieve,
With faith, our hearts will still believe.
The love we've shared can never part,
For they reside within our heart.

In moments soft, they come to gaze,
A presence felt in twilight's haze.
A hymn of hope, we sing tonight,
For those we cherish in the light.

With open arms, we set them free,
In joy and peace, eternally.
A bond unbroken, spirit's flight,
We hold them close, within our sight.

## Benediction in the Twilight

As day descends and shadows loom,
We gather now within this room.
With voices raised to heaven's ear,
We seek a blessing, calm and clear.

In twilight's glow, the spirit stirs,
With whispers soft, and gentle purrs.
May grace abound within our lives,
As we embrace the love that thrives.

Let every heart find solace here,
In unity, we conquer fear.
A benediction, sweet and warm,
In every soul, our love's the balm.

Embrace the night as it unfolds,
In stories shared, a truth retold.
May kindness grow, like flowers wild,
In every heart, forever styled.

Together we stand, hand in hand,
As twilight spreads across the land.
With hopeful hearts, we wish to see,
A world transformed, in harmony.

# **Echoing Light Beyond the Veil**

In sacred silence, echoes start,
A light that shines, a gentle heart.
Beyond the veil, they draw so near,
Invisible paths, divinely clear.

In every flicker, love's embrace,
Where weary souls may find their place.
With open arms, they welcome all,
A soft reminder, we are called.

The stars above, they twinkle bright,
A map of journeys, pure delight.
With every breath, the truth we find,
A bond unbroken through all time.

So let us walk this hallowed ground,
With spirits high, our voices sound.
A harmony that cuts through strife,
In every soul, the gift of life.

As echoes fade, we hold the light,
In hearts aflame, through day and night.
With faith as anchor, love a sail,
We find our way, beyond the veil.

# The Soul's Journey to Solace

A journey starts with each heartbeat,
A soft awakening, bittersweet.
From earthly ties, the soul takes flight,
In search of peace, through day and night.

With every step, the path unfolds,
In whispered winds, a truth retold.
Through valleys deep, and mountains high,
The spirit soars, aimed at the sky.

In sacred trust, we learn to find,
The solace dwelling in the mind.
With every tear, a lesson learned,
In every loss, a heart returns.

The stars above, like dreams of old,
Illuminate the stories told.
As night descends and peace arrives,
The soul awakens, truly thrives.

So let us walk this path with grace,
With open hearts, we'll find our place.
For every journey has its end,
But love endures, and will transcend.

## **Unfurling the Tapestry of Release**

In the quiet dawn, we kneel in prayer,
Threads of sorrow weave through the air.
The sun breaks forth, a golden embrace,
Releasing burdens with gentle grace.

Hearts uplifted, we find our way,
In shadows cast, we choose to stay.
With faith as our guide, we seek the light,
In the tapestry of love, all feels right.

Whispers of hope in the morning choir,
A chorus of souls, rising higher.
We let go of fears, we learn to trust,
In the fabric of life, it's love that must.

Each thread unique, a story spun,
Bound by the spirit, we are all one.
With each release, we grow and bloom,
In this sacred space, the light shall loom.

As we unfurl what once was tight,
The soul dances free, embracing the light.
In every ending, a new start unfolds,
In the tapestry of life, our truth is told.

# **Glistening Tears in the Sanctuary**

In the sacred hall, tears softly gleam,
Each droplet, a prayer, a whispered dream.
Beneath the arches, sorrow takes flight,
Glistening hopes wrapped in gentle light.

Amidst the silence, the heartbeats sound,
Echoes of grace in the peace we found.
With every tear, a burden released,
In the holy stillness, we are at least.

Candles flicker, illuminating the way,
For those we mourn, their spirits stay.
Each glistening tear, a love unforgot,
In the warmth of the sanctuary, we are caught.

Embrace the moments, the joy and the pain,
In every drop, a love to sustain.
We gather together, hand in hand,
In the company of grace, we take our stand.

Awash in memories, our hearts we align,
In the sanctuary's glow, our souls intertwine.
Glistening tears, a testament of faith,
In the warmth of love, we find our place.

## A Farewell Wrapped in Grace

In the softest whisper, we say goodbye,
With hearts full of love, beneath the sky.
A farewell wrapped in a shroud of grace,
In every smile, a cherished embrace.

The moments we shared, forever will gleam,
In the tapestry of life, a radiant dream.
With each step taken, we carry your light,
In the echoes of laughter, we hold you tight.

Wrapped in memories that time cannot sever,
We bid you farewell, yet love lasts forever.
In the stillness within, you softly reside,
A beacon of hope, our hearts open wide.

Though the path may part, our spirits entwine,
As we walk this journey, your legacy shines.
With tears of blessing, we honor your way,
In the grace of departure, love leads the way.

Each farewell a promise, a circle complete,
In the heart's journey, we find our heartbeat.
A farewell wrapped in love's tender embrace,
In the arms of forever, you find your place.

## The Radiance of Parting Souls

In the twilight glow, where shadows play,
The radiance shines, guiding the way.
Parting souls, like stars that ascend,
In the vastness of night, love knows no end.

With every farewell, a new journey starts,
Echoing in silence, our united hearts.
In the grace of the moment, let spirits soar,
In joy and in sorrow, we gather once more.

A shining path, where memories guide,
Through love's embrace, we shall abide.
With each gentle whisper, we feel the call,
In the radiance of love, we rise, we fall.

As daylight fades, and shadows grow long,
The parting of souls sings a timeless song.
In the softest farewell, we find our peace,
In the glow of remembrance, our love shall never cease.

In the heart of the night, light still remains,
Through all our losses, beauty sustains.
The radiance of souls, like beacons of light,
Guides us through darkness, to forever bright.

Milton Keynes UK
Ingram Content Group UK Ltd.
UKHW020039271124
451585UK00012B/935